AF261030

Dedication

I dedicate this to every hungry Christian who wants to live a better Christian life and grow close to Jesus. Scripture promises that of you obey Jesus and his commandments that Jesus will manifest himself to you. This is my prayer for you.

THE NARROW WAY

THE FIFTY COMMANDMENTS

OF JESUS

A DEVOTIONAL

MATTHEW ROBERT PAYNE

CONTENTS

Introduction

Jesus said in John 14:21, "He who has my commandments and keeps him it is he who loves me and he who loves me will be loved by my father and I will love him and manifest myself to him."

It's important to know that Jesus will manifest more of himself and even turn up in a vision, turn up in the flesh, to say hello to you if you keep these commandments, so that's a good reason to keep them.

There are two types of manifest here that I want to cover. One way that Jesus will manifest himself to you is that, as you begin to obey him and continue to obey him, is that you will develop the mind of Christ and the heart of Christ. When you are used to taking every temptation and thought captive to the commands of Jesus, you will begin to walk just as Jesus did. When you have the mind and heart of Jesus, you will truly become a delightful person.

The second meaning of manifest was the one that I was going after. I wanted to meet Jesus and, since I began obeying the Fifty Commands of Jesus and travelling the narrow way, I have had my spiritual eyes opened and I have met Jesus hundreds of times in visions. I have also met Jesus five times in the flesh, where he came out of heaven with a strange body like he appeared to Mary in the garden and the men on the road to Emmaus. This type of body needs you to discern that the person you met is actually Jesus and not another human.

Five times also, homeless people I have been friends with have gone into a trance and Jesus has had a two-way conversation with me through the body of my friend. These have been some wonderful encounters. All of these homeless people were people I loved and had shared my time and money with.

After 20 years with the fifty commandments in my possession, I have met Jesus hundreds of times on earth, countless times in heaven in visions and ten times in the flesh. The motivation to meet Jesus therefore is a very good reason to start to obey the commands of Jesus.

If Jesus loves you and the Father loves you, according to John 14:21, you can also be sure that if you obey his commands he will never say to you, *"Depart from me, I never knew you."*

Whilst I initially started to obey Jesus to meet him, I am now glad he has manifested his mind and heart to me and I am now a little Jesus. The adventures with a Savior and Lord that comes and eats with you cannot be compared to anything on earth. I compel you to this work.

Special note about Editing

In times past in most of my books that have been published previously I had a very expensive editor that I used to edit my books. My ministry income has now halved, and I cannot afford the expense for that quality of editor, so I apologize that the quality of my writing has decreased. I hope that you can appreciate my predicament and that you will still choose to read my books. If you "feel led." to sponsor the editing for a future book with a higher quality of editing, I would be open to that.

Command 1

Don't call Jesus 'Lord' when you don't obey him.

(Luke 6:46 and Matthew 7:21)

Jesus said, *"Why do you call me Lord and you do not do what I say?"* Many people know Jesus as a savior and as their friend, or what they believe is their friend, but they don't take their marching orders from Jesus. They don't obey Jesus. They certainly don't know these fifty commands, and so they don't obey Jesus in their daily life. Jesus doesn't like to be called 'Lord Jesus,' unless you're obeying him.

People don't know it, but a lord used to be an owner of property and he'd own all the people on his property - they all worked for him. The idea of Jesus being Lord in that way has ceased from people's vocabulary. They have no idea of Jesus being Lord in charge of their lives, and this needs to change if Jesus is going to be Lord.

Command 2

Build on the rock of obedience to Jesus, otherwise you will fall.

(Matthew 7:24-7, Luke 6:47-49)

Jesus taught in a sermon on the mountain many things that a Christian, a follower of Jesus, is meant to do. At the end of the sermon on the mountain he said, *"Wise is a man who listens to these things that I have said, these sayings of mine and built his life upon them. For wise is a man that is building his house on the rock, but a fool is a person who listens to these sayings of mine and does not obey them."*

Jesus was saying that you're foolish if you don't obey him and what he teaches, so these fifty commands that we're going to go through are Jesus' teachings - you need to build on the rock of obedience and obey these commands that Jesus teaches here.

Command 3

Worship God alone

(Matthew 4:10b, Luke 4:8)

When it comes to worshiping God alone, there are many people who have all sorts of idols that they worship. They worship idols with their time, with their singing and with their devotion. They buy things from the idol, they buy their idols music, they follow in the trends of the clothing of the idol and they do all sorts of things. Jesus says quite clearly in the scriptures that you should worship God alone. You should devote yourself to Jesus, devote yourself to God and not be carried away, following, chasing up and doing the actions of some idol that you admire.

Command 4

Follow Jesus

(Matthew 4:19, Matthew 11:28-30, Mark 1:17, John 1:43, John 12:26, John 10:27, John 21:22b)

Jesus used to say, *"Follow me."* A rabbi, when he was picking his indentured students, when he trained students and wanted to take on a new rabbi and teach a young boy to be a rabbi, he used to say, "Follow me." Jesus, as a rabbi, as a teacher, went around Israel and said what a rabbi says to someone when he wants him to be indentured and become a rabbi with him - he said, *"Follow me."*

We should not only be disciples of Jesus; we should follow him in all that he did and all that he said. We should have a lifestyle of obedience to what Jesus taught and we should follow his yoke. His yoke is his form of teaching, and the way that he taught the things that he taught.

One way of following Jesus is to have an understanding of these commands and obey them and understanding the parables of Jesus. You don't follow Jesus by going the opposite way; you don't follow Jesus by disobeying what he taught you. Follow Jesus by doing exactly what he taught.

Command 5

Be salt and light to the world.

(Matthew 5:13-16, Mark 9:50, Luke 11:33, Luke 14:34, John 3:21)

Jesus said quite clearly that we're not to hide our light under a basket; we're not meant to light a lamp, put it under a basket and hide our light. We're meant to display our light. Jesus said that you should put a light on a lampstand where it gives light to the whole house and the heathen will see it, see our good works and give praise to God.

Our Christian lifestyle should be a demonstration of Jesus Christ. People should not just meet a Christian, they should meet Jesus. Our lifestyle should shine light on ourselves and lead people to faith in Jesus. We shouldn't be known just as Christians; we should be known by our love and our demonstration of the character of Jesus Christ. Salt is something that preserves; salt is something that gives flavor and we should preserve society and bring flavor to society - and not so much the salt that you put onto a road and gets crushed down to handle ice.

We should be a light to the world and an example to the world, rather than something to be laughed at.

Command 6

Don't call your brother a fool.

(Matthew 5:21-22, Matthew 12:36)

It's tempting to call someone a fool. I am the first to confess that I've called people names in the past. I've called them derogatory things, called people a fool and it's important that we don't do that. Jesus teaches that we can be in danger of losing our eternal life if we do things like that, so it's important that we don't. We should deal better with people who cause us strife and do wrong towards us.

We should be in a state of forgiveness and a state of understanding. Just recently, I had a fallout with my older brother and another friend of mine. They were throwing names all around and calling me different names - and this was very disconcerting. It's actually the names that they call you that hang around after they've left. It's those accusations and names that they call you that hurt the most, rather than the relationship breaking down. Jesus is reminding us not to call each other names here and it's important not to.

Command 7

Practice instant reconciliation.

(Matthew 5:24-25)

It would be good if you can reconcile things right away with a person. Sometimes that might not be possible but having the spirit of forgiveness about you is something that's recommended. I had fallen out with one of my friends that I had talked to recently, and this verse convicted me to send them a message today.

Now I do want to tell you something about forgiveness - sometimes someone hurts you and the hurt is so large that you can't forgive them. In those instances, I find it handy to pray to the Holy Spirit and ask the Holy Spirit to give you the grace to forgive, to be able to allow you to heal to a point where you'll have the grace to be able to forgive the person.

That's something I suggest you do with deep hurts and painful things. Pray to the Holy Spirit that he would give you grace to forgive. Jesus said in Matthew 5, *"If you don't forgive your brother of evil, will you be forgiven?"* This praying for the Holy Spirit to give you grace to forgive will solve that problem and make sure you do go to heaven. You can wait until you've been healed and worked through the painful memory before you actually forgive. So, as long as you're in a state where you do want to forgive that's a good state.

Command 8

Do not look with lust at another; this is adultery in the heart.

(Matthew 5:27-28)

For all of you people who walk down the street, look at a female and wish that you could undress her and have her in bed, that's exactly what this is talking about. For all of you males and females, some females do this too, that are addicted to pornography, this is something that Jesus says is not right. You're committing spiritual adultery with a person in your heart, and Jesus says, "Stop it."

I had a long addiction, a 39-year addiction, to pornography and I know it's hard to break. You can ask someone to pray for you, confess that sin to a brother and have them pray for you to receive the grace to break out of that addiction.

Command 9

Do not divorce and marry another, this is adultery.

(Matthew 5:32, Matthew 19:9, Mark 10:11-12)

This was a real issue in Jesus' day, as people were divorcing for all sorts of reasons and remarrying. Chief among them was that Pharisees would see someone else that they desired more than their wife, and so they divorced their wife. Divorce and remarriage is an issue today, but it's not as much as an issue as it was back then. There are wives and husbands that get a no-fault divorce, they separate for a year and then get a divorce. God does not hold you accountable for divorce when there are real issues.

If you've had a partner separate from you without counselling, without restitution and without any interest in restitution - they go through the process and divorce you without your say - this verse isn't saying that you can't remarry. In the context when Jesus spoke this verse, he didn't want to allow people to do this - so this is the one of the commands that you can take notice of and don't just divorce and remarry for any reason. This is one of the commands that may not be strictly in effect as it reads today.

Command 10

Don't swear an oath.

(Matthew 5:33-37)

The scripture says, *"Let your yes be yes and your no be no."* We don't practically swear oaths today; we do have contracts and society has us doing contracts, but not many people swear an oath today. Please understand that your word is your word, and if you want to go further than that, then Jesus says that Satan is the author of going further than that. Bear that in mind, and don't make promises that you're not going to keep.

Command 11

Do more than expected; go the second mile.

(Matthew 5:38-41)

In Roman days, a Roman soldier could make you carry their equipment for a mile. They could just walk up to any person in the land and command them to carry their equipment for a mile. Jesus said when that happens to you as a disciple, carry it for two miles and make an impression on the soldier. That did make an impression. When you didn't put it down after a mile, the soldier would ask you what compels you to carry the second mile, so this impressed them in that day.

This should be our discipline as a beautiful Christian and being an example. When someone asks you to do something, go the second mile - just go over and above what they ask for and this allows you to be a great witness to people.

I talk more about being salt and light in my books: *Influencing Your World for Christ* and *13 Tips to Becoming the Light of Christ.'* These are two books that I've written that talk about how to be light, and this is one of the things covered in those books.

Command 12

Give to those who ask.

(Matthew 5:42, Luke 6:30, 38)

Give to people who ask is a commandment that I learned to do early on when I originally had the list of fifty commands. There was a list of forty commands that I had, and my mother increased it to fifty commands. The top 40 is what a group called *The Jesus Christians* presented, a tract that listed the commands of Jesus. I started to give to those who asked for change and, because I couldn't remember all the commands, I just did this one. When homeless people ask you for money with a sign on the street or they cry out to you and ask you, then this commandment is saying, "Give them your spare change."

One of the commandments is, 'Give to those who ask and from those who steal from you don't require it back.' Someone who's desperate will steal, but Jesus says, "Let them steal from you and don't try and get your goods back." Let them have the money that they got from it. Another of the commandments is, "Give to those who ask and don't turn away those who want to borrow from you."

Jesus is pretty insistent about giving and I have found that you may say to yourself that if you just keep on giving away spare change, you'll never have spare change. I've personally found that when I didn't have any change left, or I couldn't afford to give any more out, that the people stopped asking me. The Holy Spirit stopped impressing them to ask me, so you're never going to be at a position where you haven't got enough money to give.

I really encourage you, if you're going through this book in the future, to start to carry some change and start to give, and you'll see your whole life turn around.

Command 13

Love, bless and pray for your enemies.

(Matthew 5:43-48, Luke 6:27-29)

If someone becomes an enemy, such as someone you know gives you a barrage of insults and has made it their life mission to cause you trouble, you need to love, bless and pray for them. I've found personally in my life that when you start to pray for an enemy (and I haven't had many in my life) you start to feel engaged in the prayer. The more time and effort you put into the prayers for your enemy, the more your heart is softened towards them and it's in the process of praying for your enemy that you'll forgive them.

Your heart will change towards them, so that the animosity is only going one way - from you there's love going towards them. From them, there's hate coming towards you - and this is a good way to process your pain. This is a good way for you to be postured towards your enemies and coming from your side is only peace.

Command 14

Quietly do good for God's praise alone.

(Matthew 6:1– 4)

It's important as a Christian to do your good works without boasting, without letting the whole world know about what you're doing. When you're giving alms, for instance, when you're giving to the poor, do it in such a way that people can't see you doing it. When you're giving to a charity, don't announce it - don't have them on a telephone announcing your name, but make a stipulation that you don't want it announced. You just want to give, and so Jesus compels you to give.

Take heed that you do not do your good deeds before men to be seen by them, otherwise you have no reward from your Father in heaven - that's what Matthew 6:1 says. So do your good works in private and you'll be blessed by God in public.

Command 15

When you pray, fast or give, do it secretly.

(Matthew 6:5-6)

Jesus is continuing on the theme - when you pray, fast or give, do it privately. So, when you pray, go into your private room and pray. Jesus commands that when you fast, don't make a big show of the fact that you're fasting. Oftentimes when you're fasting someone will ask you, "Do you want a meal?" or "Why aren't you eating?"

Sometimes you have to say, "I'm fasting." It always seems to be the case when I'm fasting that someone asks me "Why are you not eating?" You can say that if it comes up but try and arrange your fast for times when you're not going to be going out for dinner. And when you're giving, like the commandment before, give in secret.

When you're doing religious things, when you're praying, fasting and giving, make sure that you do it in private so there's no reward from people and there's no people's opinions that you're particularly religious. Jesus will reward you in public; and the Father will reward you in public.

Command 16

Don't use vain repetitions when praying.

(Matthew 6:7-8, Matthew 12:40)

I've never been part of an institution that uses vain repetitions. You could almost say that the Lord's Prayer is one of them; it's just the same prayer over and over and over again. I respect people in the Catholic tradition that say the Lord's Prayer over and over again, but be conscious. If you're part of that tradition, just be conscious that Jesus said this and try to make the Lord's Prayer fresh every time to yourself, rather than just something you know by rote.

I've never personally been part of something that uses vain repetition in prayer, but you can take a serious note that Jesus doesn't approve. Apparently, I had a friend who is dating a Jew, and the Jews are very good at doing vain repetitions and long lengthy prayers - and Jesus spoke against it. There's no picking on Jews - Jesus was a Jew himself, and so this may be why he was saying it.

Command 17

Pray to God the Father.

(Matthew 6:9, John 16:23-24)

Jesus commands us in those verses to pray to God the Father. I pray to the Father quite a lot, but I also pray to Jesus and I direct my prayers to Jesus. I don't do what people would typically call a prayer. I'll just have conversations and that's a good practice to get yourself into having conversations with God. When you pray, Jesus compels or commands us to pray to his Father, so I encourage you to do that - be blessed in doing that and be blessed as the Father answers your prayers.

Command 18

Don't be anxious.

(Matthew 6:25-32, Luke 12:22-30, John 14:1, John 16:33)

Jesus has said it a number of times here, or the disciples have recorded it a number of times - don't be anxious. It's so tempting to be anxious, and it's such a programmed response that we have to be anxious. I'm doing this book during the coronavirus and there are a lot of people who are anxious about that; it's important to not worry and instead to pray. I've got a saying that I say to myself when I catch myself worrying - *don't worry, pray* - so whenever you catch yourself worrying, stop your worrying and pray to Jesus with your burden. Pray to God that the burden would be lifted and the thing you are worrying about would be solved; that'll keep you from being anxious.

Command 19

Store your riches in heaven not on earth.

(Matthew 6:19-21,33, Luke 12:21, 31-34, John 12:12-23)

It's important for you to find out how to store your riches in heaven. Many people have no idea how to. I can say quite simply that whenever you're financing people to become a Christian, whenever people are being fed, whenever the poor are being serviced, you're storing your riches towards heaven if you're helping in that.

Whenever you're financing someone to grow in intimacy or become closer to Jesus, you're storing your riches in heaven. There are many ministries that you can support to help store your riches in heaven. This is about not having Nike shoes, Nike pants, Prada and all the best brand-names and all the best possessions on earth. Jesus is saying spend your money, not so much on all the best brands for yourself, but spend your money on the kingdom.

I'd encourage you to stop spending so much on yourself and start investing your finances into the kingdom of God. There's so much idolatry in the world and so many people are idolizing the world and its lust. It's just important that people learn to store their riches in heaven, and it's important that they learn how to do that. I'd encourage you to do some research on the internet on how to store your riches in heaven, because I can say a large percentage of Christians just don't do it.

24

Command 20

Judge not that you may not be judged.

(Matthew 7:1-5, Luke 6:37, Luke 6:41-42, John 7:24)

It's important that you understand the commandments of God, and it's important that you understand what's expected by God - but it's often important for you not to judge people. Paul said that no one judges him, and he doesn't even judge himself, and it's important that you live a life where you're not judging. It's not our position to put a teaching up on YouTube about certain ministries that aren't preaching the gospel; we're not called to be the accuser of the brethren.

It's important that you allow people to be themselves; you can take people aside and suggest things, and you can take people aside and encourage them to go a different way. But as for judging people, Jesus was clear about not judging. He said clearly to take the speck out of your own eye before you judge. You'll find if you do an investigation into yourself that there's enough wrong with yourself, before you'll ever get around to judging other people.

It's an important point - it's important to not to be fault-finding in other people, but it's more important for you to be introspective and looking at yourself. And when you're doing everything right and perfect, rather than calling people out and judging people, just come alongside them and give them suggestions and encouragements to change - don't be so outright and judge them.

Command 21

Keep asking and knocking.

(Matthew 6:9-11, Matthew 7:7-11, Luke 11:9-13)

It's vital that we learn to ask Jesus for things and ask the Father for things. Many of us, if you're anything like me, have low self-esteem and we don't feel worthy of things - and so some of us, like myself, aren't particularly used to asking for things. But James 2:3 says, *"You have not because you asked not,"* so James makes it clear that we don't have things because we don't ask for them. And Jesus compels us in these commandments to keep asking, keep knocking and seeking things - so we're commanded to ask and so we should ask. We should get over ourselves and have the ability to ask our Savior for things.

Command 22

Treat others as you like to be treated.

(Matthew 7:12, Luke 6:31)

Everyone likes to be treated with love and in a cordial way, and we should do unto others as we would like them to do unto us. It's important to treat others with respect and with love. It's not okay to insult someone, it's not okay to pick on someone, it's not okay to fight back; we're told to turn the other cheek and to pray for our enemies. It's not okay for you to spitefully treat people and be mean towards people, or be spiteful in any way. What you're meant to do is treat other people the way that you'd like to be treated - which is totally different to how some people treat other people.

Command 23

Don't waste time on argumentative people.

(Matthew 7:6)

I had a friend who I spoke to and I told him that he lacks integrity, and that I'm not going to be going out and witnessing with him anymore. He was calling me all sorts of names and wanted to enter into a tit-for-tat sort of argument over Facebook messenger. The Holy Spirit said, "Don't even write back to him." Some people with different spirits affecting their lives like to argue; they have real fun arguing. I've had that spirit in myself, so I know that it causes arguments and loves to argue. Jesus commands us not to argue with those people, and if we find that spirit in ourselves to find a deliverance from that spirit. If anything in you likes to argue, you need to be delivered - so don't waste your time on argumentative people.

Command 24

Forgive others.

(Matthew 6:12, 6:14-15, 6:18-21, Mark 11:5-26, Luke 11:9-13)

It's mentioned five times there to forgive others, so I feel that Jesus is very insistent that we forgive others. It's very much on the top of Christ's agenda and Jesus typified this as he hung on the cross when he said, *"Father, forgive them that they know not what they do."* Jesus, in the midst of his torturous and painful crucifixion, was ending his life in forgiveness; he's able to teach on forgiveness because in excruciating pain he forgave the people that hurt him. He couldn't die in unforgiveness because then he would have sin, so he cleansed himself of his pain and he forgave the people who killed him on the cross as an example that we too should forgive other people.

Command 25

Let the dead bury the dead.

(Matthew 8:22, Luke 9:6a)

It was the job of an older brother in Jewish families of Jesus' day, the eldest son in a family, to bury his parents - and when he buried his parents, the inheritance would pass on to him. So, when the person said to Jesus that he had to bury his dad, he was saying that he wouldn't get his inheritance unless he did that thing. And Jesus was saying "Hey, let other people bury your father. You come with me - don't worry about your inheritance." So that's what "let the dead bury their dead" actually means. It means that when you follow Jesus, don't count on other sources of income.

Don't be going to the world for your sustenance; but when you've got an invitation to follow Jesus and you get an invitation by the Holy Spirit, follow the Holy Spirit's invitation - don't be thinking about money. You could also say let the unbeliever worry about the unbeliever, or let the dead church worry about the dead church; don't worry about what people who are religious say about you - let the dead bury the dead. That could be true also of this verse, but it mainly speaks towards provision - let a work of faith be a work of faith, not something that you need guaranteed income for.

Command 26

Don't fear people, fear God.

(Matthew 10:28, Matthew 16:23, Luke 12:4-5)

This is a really difficult one for me, because we tend to fear people and we tend to fear what people think of us. In countries overseas we find that people are fearful of the government and are fearful of what governments can do to them. In the United States right now, there are a whole lot of riots and walking the streets, and there's fear. Jesus' commandment here is not to fear people but to fear God. It may be difficult to walk in, but it's always important to obey Jesus and take his word. Jesus says don't fear what men can do to you, fear what God can do to you. And so, it's important to get some perspective - but we have to confess that fear is something that comes natural to us and so it may be difficult for you to obey this one. You certainly may need the help of the Holy Spirit to obey this commandment.

Command 27

Confess Christ before men.

(Matthew 10:32-33, Mark 5:19, Mark 8:38, Luke 9:26, Luke 12:8-9)

It's important to confess that Jesus is part of your life, it's important to confess Jesus, and it's important to witness in Jesus' name. What I have found more effective and more important is to be Jesus to people. If someone needs money, give them money; if someone needs help moving to a new house, help them move to a new house; if someone's sick take them some food; if someone needs someone to listen to them, listen to them.

In being Jesus to people, people will ask you questions while you're doing what you're doing - and that's when you confess Christ and that's when you say Jesus compels me to do this. So, there's a lot of people trying to witness and preaching Christ at people - sometimes that's okay, but sometimes it's said in a spirit of religion and a lot of people out there witnessing have got religious spirits. So, it's important to demonstrate the character of Jesus before you go preaching at people.

Command 28

Take up your cross.

(Matthew 10:38-39, Matthew 16 24-26, Matthew 8:34-37, Luke 9:23-26, Luke 14:26-33)

When people were crucified, part of the punishment was for them to carry the cross. It wasn't just carrying the beam of the cross, which was hard to carry, but it was the marching through the streets in front of the people. The people used to hiss at them, scream at them, spit on them and curse them and so it was not only a hard journey carrying the plank of wood but it was also a hard journey because there was the spitting and the shouting and the jeering of the people. When Jesus says, *"Take up your cross,"* we're to live the life of a Christian - we're to live the life and daily die to self, and daily take up our cross.

Sometimes you have to do something that you don't really want to do - for instance, waking up today and being told by the Holy Spirit to do this series on the commandments. This is very hard on me and it's taking a while to do it. The video that this was made from, the part 1, was 37 minutes and I'm only at 28 minutes in part 2. I'm only just a bit past halfway, so taking up your cross often is doing something that's hard – it's doing something that your flesh resists, but Jesus says to do it anyway. So, taking up your cross is obeying Jesus, and obeying the leading of the Holy Spirit - it can be hard, and it can mean people mock you.

Command 29

Beware of hypocrisy and greed.

(Matthew 15:6-9, Matthew 23:28, Luke 6:41-42, 12:1b, Luke 20:46-47).

Hypocrisy is a major thing in the Christian church. The Christian church tends to have all sorts of rules and have all sorts of things that they tell people that they need to do. They tend to point the finger at everyone else but themselves; but when it comes to obeying Jesus and being like Jesus, they're hypocrites - and Jesus says beware of hypocrisy. He also says to beware of greed in these verses, and I certainly know that many Christians are greedy and selfish, and they pursue the things of the world more than they pursue Jesus - this is a problem. So, hypocrisy is one thing the Christian church can be accused of in telling other people how to live their life, and yet we don't live our life like Christ.

The Christian church is certainly full of people who are motivated by greed, and you can see the combination of hypocrisy and greed in the prosperity preachers and the preachers that get on TV.

Command 30

Privately rebuke a brother and if he repents, forgive him.

(Matthew 18:5, Luke 17:3-4)

This means not to publicly rebuke a brother. Jesus encourages us to privately rebuke your brother and, if he repents, forgive him. This would almost mean that you shouldn't be doing public videos on people's ministries to rebuke them and call them out as a false prophet. The proper spiritual order would be to write to the person privately to bring the accusations and the rebuke to the person, rather than do a public video. But the thing is that people say they can't get through to the email address, and they won't receive what they're saying, and so they publicly rebuke a person - and that's just not on.

Also, in person-to-person sort of situations, rather than speaking badly in the lunchroom about someone who did something to you, the Lord wants you to privately go to the person who said something or did something to you and privately rebuke them. The Lord says approach them privately, say that you didn't like what they did and ask them to say sorry - rather than publicly going into the lunchroom and spouting off about what they did, and having the people in the lunchroom come against the person.

That's normally the way that people do it at work - they go into the lunchroom and tell everyone what a bad thing such and such did; and that works, because the person comes into the lunchroom and they're shamed by everyone. They come and say sorry to you, to try and make up their relationship with their friends - but even though it works, it's not the right way to do things.

Command 31

Pay your taxes and give to God what is his.

(Matthew 22:21, Mark 12:17, Luke 20:25, Lk 21:4)

Jesus says give your taxes to Caesar. Jesus commands us to pay our taxes, so it's never ever right that you don't pay your taxes. So, get that straight - whatever your taxes are you should be paying them. In business you've got laws that say that you can write certain amount of expenses off and claim deductions - and that's fine; you work within your taxation laws, but pay your taxes.

More importantly you should give to God what is his. That's something that so many Christians don't do - the Lord is worthy of your tithe, and the Lord is worthy of your giving. You certainly don't store up riches in heaven, which is one of the other commandments, if you don't give to God. People can argue all day to say that tithing is in the Old Testament it's not a New Testament thing, but this commandment tells you to give God his dues.

In the New Testament, we're shown plenty on giving and Paul says that people who give generously are rewarded generously, and we shouldn't hold back our giving to God. I'm a person who gives a lot to God. Up to 20% of my income goes to other ministries, and I encourage you also to learn how to give to God.

Michael Van Vlymen, a good friend of mine, has got a good book on giving called *Supernatural Provision: Learning to Walk in Greater Levels of Stewardship and Responsibility and Letting Go of Unbiblical Beliefs* - and Andrew Wommack has got a good book on giving called *Financial Stewardship*. That's a good book on giving, and I encourage you to give.

Command 32

Love God and others.

(Matthew 22:37-40, Mark 12:30-31, Luke 10:27, John 15:12, John 13:34-35)

It's important to love people, and it's important to love God and others. The two greatest commandments are to love God with all your heart, mind and soul, and love others just as Christ loved you. If you love God, you'll give to God; if you love others, you'll give to God where it's helping other people; if you don't love God and love others, you won't be giving a tremendous amount. If you love yourself, if you love everything about yourself, you'll be sowing up your riches on earth and you won't be sowing up your riches in heaven. Do you see how these all tie in together? So loving God and others not only involves investing time in getting to know God and getting to know other people, but it involves your resources, it involves your money, it involves every part of you.

It's important that you just don't tell people that you love them, but you demonstrate your love for other people. That can be done through acts of service, that can be done with time spent, that can be done with giving them things that can be done by providing for their needs. There are so many ways to demonstrate the love of Jesus with people. I've mentioned my two books and I'd encourage you to read *13 Tips to Becoming the*

Light of Christ" or *Influencing Your World for Christ*. These are two books that will encourage you how to live the Godly life.

Command 33

Keep alert and watch for the second coming.

(Matthew 24:44, 46, 50-51, Mark 14:62, Luke 12:35-40, 21:27-28)

It's important to be aware that Jesus is coming again. Michael L. Brown has written a book called *Not Afraid* and that's a book that I encourage you to buy because in that book he teaches that the second coming and the rapture are the same event. It teaches that all of us are going to go through the tribulation and need to be prepared for the tribulation, so part of this commandment is to be alert and watch. Jesus shares parables about being alert and watching, and he talks about the thief breaking in at a time when people weren't aware - the thief breaking in is a symbol for the day of the Lord. The day of the Lord is a day of judgment, trial and chastisement by God - and that's going to come before the second coming. So, you need to be alert and watch, and be ready for the trials coming to earth.

Command 34

Honor God with all that you have been given.

(Matthew 25:14-31, Luke 18:18)

Jesus says here to honor God with all you've been given; honor God with your time, with your finances, with your personality, with your love. Honoring God is not only worshiping God but giving him your tithes and sponsoring his work on earth. You honor God by honoring other people.

There's love that goes vertical, that's the love between you and God, and then there's love that goes horizontal - that's the love between you and other people. When Jesus put his arms out on the cross it was a horizontal love; there's one part of the cross going vertical, he was doing a sacrifice for his Father, but his arms were horizontal - which means he was dying for us. We need to honor God by not only worshiping him with our mouths and with our actions, but we also need to honor people and love people - and that's a good way to honor God.

Command 35

Minister to others as you would to Jesus himself.

(Matthew 25:34-46)

Jesus wants us to treat other people like we would treat him, and Jesus wants us to be encouraging, he wants us to be loving, he wants us to be giving, he wants us to be compassionate. He wants us to be forgiving, he wants us to be merciful, he wants us to love without condition, and he wants us to love people without keeping a record of what we're doing. So how would you minister to Jesus? What would you do for Jesus himself? So many people walk past the poor, the hungry, the thirsty, the people with dirty clothes, the homeless on the street, and deny them food and drink and shelter and new clothes - and Jesus says not to do this in the parable of the sheep and the goats which this reference talks about.

You should demonstrate your love to other people like you demonstrate your love to Jesus himself, and so many people fail this one because they just don't care about anyone. They certainly don't care about the poor, and Jesus says that's not right. Jesus says you should minister to people as though you're ministering to him and he says in fact that when you do that, you are ministering to him. So, every time you've given money to a homeless person, every time you've given a poor person a drink, you've been giving to the Lord himself.

Command 36

Preach the gospel and teach obedience.

(Matthew 28:20, Mark 16:15, Luke 9:60b, John 21:15b,16b,17b)

One thing that I teach is obedience - I teach obedience to Jesus, these very commandments what you need to obey, and in my 57 books I've endeavored to preach the gospel. The gospel is not living for the world but living for Jesus and demonstrating Jesus to everyone that you know. How you demonstrate Jesus is you obey these commandments. So, preaching the gospel isn't always getting out on the street and saying you need to repent and follow Jesus; you can preach the gospel more effectively than on the street just by going up to all the homeless and giving them a cold drink.

You can preach the gospel by being the gospel on the streets for sure. So many people assume that preaching the gospel is opening your mouth, but sometimes the best way to preach the gospel isn't to open your mouth - sometimes preaching the gospel is best demonstrated by acts of love and obedience. Jesus compels us to obey him, and he even tells us that we need to obey him. You can better obey Jesus by reading my companion book *THE NARROW WAY - The Parables of Jesus Made Simple 2021 Edition.*

Command 37

Repent of your sins.

(Mark 1:15, Luke 13:3,5, Luke 15:7,10,18,24)

Jesus compels us to repent of our sins, and that means when you know that you're doing wrong the only way to do right is to come to a place where you're sorry for your sin and you're ready to turn away from your sin. Repent doesn't mean I say "Sorry" and repent doesn't mean "Please forgive me, Jesus," repent means "Please forgive me Jesus, and I'm never going to do it again - give me the grace never to do it again, and I won't be doing it again." To repent is turn around, change your mind, and change the way you do things differently. So many Christians are repeating their sins all the time, and that's not what repentance is. I'll share that I had an addiction to pornography for 39 years and I found it very hard to find a place of repentance - so it's not that I don't understand people who are stuck in sin. It's not that Jesus doesn't understand people, because it took a long time for me to find the grace to walk free. But repenting of your sins isn't just words, it's action.

I feel so wonderful to be so free right now; I had a couple of sex addictions and it's so wonderful to walk free of them. My prayer for you is that you can address your sins, come before Jesus and ask for the grace to walk free of them. And I pray this day that you'll be free of those sins.

Command 38

Believe in Jesus.

(Mark 16:16, Luke 9:35, John 12:36, 6:29, 20:29, 14:6)

John 14:6 says, *"I am the way, the truth and the life; no one comes to the Father except through me."* Believing in Jesus isn't saying, "I believe Jesus was the son of God." Believing in Jesus is more than just saying, "Jesus is the son of God" or "Jesus is the savior" or "Jesus is my savior." Believing in Jesus is obeying Jesus - believing in Jesus is an action word. When Jesus says, *"I am the way, the truth and the life"* he is the truth that you need to follow, he is the way that you're meant to go. his way is the pedestrian crossing of life.

His ways, his commands, his directions are the way to go; his truth is the truth, his way is the truth and his life is the life you should be living - his life is the way you should follow. *"Any man who wants to come after me must deny himself, take up his cross and follow me."* You need to follow Jesus, to believe in Jesus; you don't get saved by just believing that Jesus was the son of God - you get saved by practicing what Jesus taught. It's very important for you to realize, and I'll say it very clearly here, to believe in Jesus is to obey Jesus. So, I encourage you to learn to obey him.

Command 39

Have childlike faith.

(Mark 10:15, Luke 18:17, Matthew 9:29)

This is a gift - having a childlike faith is a gift. Having childlike faith as an adult is having the ability to have a really simple faith. You can understand theological issues and you can understand complex things that are said in the scriptures, and still have childlike faith. Childlike faith is having the ability just to trust the Word of God and believe in the promises of God. I think it's possible to develop childlike faith; I think that if you went and got a book on the promises of God, and started to meditate on the promises of God, and started to believe the promises of God, that you could develop childlike faith. Jesus commands you to have childlike faith, so he wouldn't command something that isn't possible. But I consider childlike faith is found in the promises of God. If you can develop faith in the promises of God instead of faith in this world, and faith in religion, and faith in what is taught in church, if you can develop childhood faith to believe the promises of God, that would be a wonderful thing.

Command 40

Don't sell your things in God's house.

(Mark 11:15-17, John 2:16)

The practice of holding up a book and saying, "I'm going to give this book away" and holding up another book saying, "I'm going to give this book away," is a clever marketing technique. Do you know that people run competitions where they give a holiday away to collect a whole lot of names of people that want that holiday? They contact them and they sell to those people. Their names and their numbers that they enter into to be part of the competition, they use to ring them up, tell them they didn't win and then sell to them. They sell the holiday trip because people put their hand up to say they want to win it, which means that they want it. Someone holding up a book in a church and saying they're going to give away a couple of copies makes everyone in the church want that book.

When they don't get the book for free, a percentage of them go out to the book table and buy it. That's a type of marketing, but it's a terrible form of marketing and it shouldn't be done in the church. We don't have to spend too much time talking about this one, because you know when people are selling things in the church and they shouldn't do it. It's quite alright to mention your books and give away a couple of books, but don't be going through the practices of the way that they do professional marketing in the church.

50

Command 41

Rejoice when you are persecuted.

(Luke 6:22-23)

This is a hard one - when James says to have joy in your trials, that's a hard one, and this one's a hard one also. No-one enjoys being persecuted; I certainly didn't enjoy my brother saying all these bad names about me and insulting me. I certainly didn't like my former friend calling me all sorts of names. Interestingly enough, they both insulted me with the idea that I was fat. I don't find that a real insult, actually, because I know that I am fat. Interestingly, they both came out with that as though that was going to really hurt - but persecution isn't just getting called names.

Persecution is losing a job, getting passed over for promotion, having people gossip about you, having people hit you and abuse you, and really hurt you. We've got the example of the disciples who were singing in the prison after they had just been whipped; they were singing in the prison and praising God, so that's an example of rejoicing when you're persecuted. They would have remembered that from Jesus' day, when he was teaching this. So, when you are persecuted, Jesus compels us to put on a spirit of praise.

When you're persecuted, that puts you in a great frame of mind to be able to press on and persevere. So, rejoicing isn't so much "I'm so happy I got persecuted" because that's a great thing, rejoicing is changing your frame of mind so that you can handle the persecution more. Jesus said in Matthew also, *"Rejoice when you are persecuted"* - all the true prophets got persecuted in the Bible, and so you can be sure persecution will come to those people who are truly God's.

Command 42

Don't be distracted from hearing God's word.

(Luke 10:38-42)

This passage is when Martha was being distracted - she was cooking in the house and Mary was sitting at Jesus' feet. And so, Jesus is saying don't let anything distract you from hearing Jesus. So, if there's a preacher preaching, don't be looking at your phone and flipping through Facebook; if someone's preaching on YouTube, don't be doing something different. Many people turn on an audiobook or turn on YouTube and play it while they wash up and stuff - and that's fine because you want something to happen while you're washing up, and you are listening. Be careful not to be distracted when the Word of God is going forth.

I had my good friend Shayne listen to the video on this point and he shared with me that a prominent preacher rebuked him once for looking at his Facebook when he was preaching. We all can get bored. We should not be too busy to hear God, or busy doing something else when the Word is going forth.

Command 43

Act with compassion and not prejudice towards others.

(Luke 10:30-37)

This passage is the parable of 'The Good Samaritan. It's not explicitly laid out in what it says here, but we're meant as Christians to move in compassion. If you can just walk past the homeless on the street and not care for them, you haven't got compassion - you've lost your compassion. I've been told that it's pretty hard on some of the American streets as there are a lot of homeless - you can stop for one, you can stop and give one two dollars, you can stop and buy one a Coke. Don't harden your heart towards other people, Jesus says just have compassion, just as how you love your brother and sister. Jesus said we should love our neighbors and the guy asked who our neighbors were - so he told the Parable of The Good Samaritan and he said, *"Go and do likewise."* How many of you stop for that broken person on the street? How many of you are actually doing that? That's what acting in compassion is.

Command 44

Invite the poor to eat with you.

(Luke 14:13-14)

It's important to have a spirit of hospitality about you. You may not have a party and invite the poor and the maimed and the crippled to your party - Jesus told a parable about that. There are not many people that would do that, but you can certainly stop with a homeless or a poor person and buy them a drink or something to eat. You can even buy a couple of drinks and sit down with a homeless person and have a conversation.

I have heard that most homeless people feel invisible because so many people don't look at them, they don't meet them in the eye. People don't even look at them. If you were walking down the street and no one looked at you, or you were sitting down and no-one walked past looking at you and everyone turned their eyes away, you'd really start to feel invisible and hopeless after a while - and that's how homeless people are. So, if you stopped and bought a couple of drinks, and sat down and drank with them and had a conversation, you'll do more for them. You don't have to take them home, you don't have to restore them, you don't have to do anything - just love them; I encourage you to do so.

Command 45

Humble yourself and take the lowest position.

(Luke 14:8-11, 18:13-14, Matthew 23:12, 19:30)

Jesus told the parable about a man who, instead of taking a low position in the feast and sitting at the lower seat, he took the highest seat - and Jesus said "What would happen if the master of the feast came and got you and demoted you from where you sat - that would really embarrass you." Jesus said when you go to a feast to take the lowest position - it's important to be humble, and it's important to walk around in the spirit of humility.

Even though I've been preaching these commandments for eight years, this is the first time I've actually gone through them and taught them. The Holy Spirit led me to do that, but I don't go around boasting everywhere that I follow the fifty commandments of Jesus - I don't put myself in an attitude of boasting. I could say that I obey Jesus in every way, but I don't boast. I take a position where, even as I explain them, I mention how I've sinned and how I've done wrong; for example, saying that I'm going to write to my friend and say sorry for the argument the other day. That's a humble position. That's not only being convicted by this scripture that I'm teaching, but also admitting to you that I've done wrong and I'm in a wrong position - so it's important to humble yourself.

By the time I went to apologize to David, he had blocked me - so I had to write him an email!

Command 46

You must be born again.

(John 3:3, John 3:5-8)

It's important that you lead people into a prayer of salvation, and it's important that people make a decision to follow Jesus, to live for Jesus and to obey Jesus. It's important that if you're going to be the person that leads someone to follow Jesus, it's important that you're a new creation. It's important that you're obeying Jesus and you're a proper demonstration of Jesus to the person you're leading to become born-again. First of all, it's important for you to obey these commands before you start converting someone else. But if you're not born-again, you need to ask Jesus to be the savior of your life, forgive your sins and dedicate your life to Jesus.

Command 47

Live in me and live in my love.

(John 8:31-32, John 15:4,9)

Jesus says to be partnered with him and be a part of who he is, but he also says to obey him and be one with him - obey and let his Word live in you. So not only live in his love, but also live in his Word and abide in his love - and that's what the scriptures say: that you need to abide in him, and abiding is obeying. My mother, who typed up these commands, might have got that terminology wrong, but abiding in the love of Jesus is obeying the commands of Jesus; make sure that you not only love Jesus, but you obey him.

Command 48

Don't covet your brother's blessing.

(Luke 12:13-15, 15:29-30)

Luke chapter 12:13-15 is where two people were fighting over an inheritance. In my family, we've got an example of an inheritance coming up in our family - and my older brother is upset at the moment because his former wife is getting half of his portion. He got really out of sorts, because instead of getting $80,000 like the other three siblings, he is only getting $40,000 and his former wife is getting $40,000. He is really argumentative and really abusive over it, so that's an example. In that day, someone was coming to Jesus upset over an inheritance and they wanted to have Jesus judge on it.

The same is true in today with my brother getting upset over an inheritance and money tends to do that. The Prodigal Son's older brother was jealous of the younger brother getting a fatted calf put on the sacrifice for him and a party being made so don't be upset with what your Christian brother or what someone else has got. Just be happy with what you have and don't be jealous of other people's goods or other people's blessings.

Command 49

Be baptized.

(Matthew 29:19, Mark 16:16)

Jesus commands us here to be baptized - and we should be baptized in water and we should be baptized in the Holy Spirit. I don't feel that it's essential to be baptized in the Holy Spirit; I still feel that you can go to heaven. I still feel that you can go to heaven if you're not baptized in water also, but being baptized in water is good symbolism and a good way to show your friends you are saved. It is certainly a really good evangelistic opportunity to invite your non-Christian friends and family to the ceremony, so that they can see that from this day on you're going to serve Jesus.

I invited my former wife and she didn't come, but I was very happy to be baptized when I was at 27. Jesus commands us to be baptized, so that's a good reason to be baptized.

Command 50

Strive for perfection.

(Matthew 5:48, John 15:14)

Jesus said, *"Be perfect as your Father in Heaven is perfect."* So, if you live according to these commandments in this short book, if you learn these commandments, if you meditate on these commandments and put these commandments into practice, you will find that you're living a life that approaches perfection. Whilst we may never be perfect on earth, we can certainly be perfect in the righteousness of Christ. So, I hope you're encouraged by this and I hope that you feel led to share it with your friends.

Closing Words.

I encourage you to get the companion book to this book called *THE NARROW WAY: The Parables of Jesus Made Simple 2021 Edition.* These two books are being produced and edited at the same time, and it is hoped by November 2020 they will be both available on Amazon. It is my hope that most people will buy them both to complement each other as a very exhaustive source of the Narrow Way that Jesus preached in his gospel.

May you be blessed.

I'd Love to Hear from You

One of the ways that you can bless me as a writer is by writing an honest and candid review of my book on Amazon where you purchased this book. I always read the reviews of my books, and I would love to hear what you have to say about this one.

Before I buy a book, I read the reviews first. You can make an informed decision about a book when you have read enough honest reviews from readers. One way to help me sell this book and to give me positive feedback is by writing a review for me. It doesn't cost you a thing but helps me and the future readers of this book enormously.

To read my blog, request a life-coaching session, request your own personal prophecy, or receive a personal message from your angel, you can also visit my website at http://personal-prophecy-today.com. All of the funds raised through my ministry website will go toward the books that I write and self-publish.

To write to me about this book or to share any other thoughts, please feel free to contact me at my personal email address at survivors.sanctuary@gmail.com.

You can also friend request me on Facebook at Matthew Robert Payne. Please send me a message if we have no friends in common, as a lot of scammers now send me friend requests..

You can also do me a huge favor and share this book on Facebook as a recommended book to read. This will help me and other readers.

Please do not be afraid to contact me and connect with me. I enjoy speaking my readers and all my best friends have read most of my books over time. I can't contact you as I don't know who you are, but you can contact me ☺

How to Sponsor a Book Project

If you have been blessed by this book, you might consider sponsoring a book for me. It normally costs me at least $1,200 to $1500 to produce each book that I write, depending on the length of the book.

If you seek the Holy Spirit about financing a book for me, I know that the Lord would be eternally grateful to you. Consider how much this book has blessed you, and then think of hundreds or even thousands of people who would be blessed by a book of mine. As you are probably aware, the vast majority of my e-books are ninety-nine cents, which proves to you that book writing is indeed a ministry for me and not a money-making venture. I would be very happy if you supported me in this.

If you have any questions for me or if you want to know what projects I am currently working on that your money might finance, you can write to me at survivors.sanctuary@gmail.com and ask me for more information. I would be pleased to give you additional details about my projects. I have currently 5 books that I need funds to publish.

You can sow any amount to my ministry by simply sending me money via the PayPal link at this address: http://personal-prophecy-today.com/support-my-ministry.

You can be sure that your support, no matter the amount, will be used for the publishing of helpful Christian books for people to read.

About Matthew Robert Payne

Matthew Robert Payne, a teacher and prophet, enjoys writing what the Lord puts on his heart to share. He receives great pleasure from interacting with others on Facebook, hearing from people who have read his books, and prophesying over people's lives. He is a passionate lover of and disciple of Jesus Christ. He hopes that as you discover his books, you will intimately come to know Jesus, the Father, and Matthew through his transparent writing style.

Matthew grew up in a traditional Baptist church and gave his heart to Jesus Christ at the tender age of eight years old. But he left home at the age of eighteen, living a wild life for many years and engaging in bad habits and addictions. At twenty-seven, he was baptized in water and, at the same time, baptized in the Holy Spirit. Matthew learned about the five-fold ministry offices and received a revelation of their value today.

He started his journey as a prophet twenty years ago, learning about this gift and putting it into practice. With thousands of prophecies under his belt, he can confidently prophesy to friends and strangers alike. He has been writing for a number of years and self-published his first book in 2011. Today he spends his time earning money to self-publish and writes a new book approximately every month. He also produces many videos that you can view on YouTube.

You can connect with him on Facebook. You can sow into his book-writing ministry, read his blog, receive a message from your angel, or even receive your own nine-minute personal prophecy from Matthew at http://personal-prophecy-today.com.

Acknowledgments

I want to thank Jesus, the Holy Spirit, the Father, my scribe angel Bethany for the knowledge and wisdom in this book. I want to thank all of the above for the finances also as well as people who support me in ministry.

I want to thank my friends Mary, Shayne, Dundy, Lisa and others who support me with their love. Your love is priceless to me, a broken man.

I want to thank everyone else who has been used to encourage me and support me in friendship, prayer and finances. I want to especially thank those who choose to make a monthly support to my ministry and John who makes a donation every 2 weeks. This really helps me.